P9-BIG-575

Elgar

THE GREAT COMPOSERS

ELGAR

by

MICHAEL HURD

FABER AND FABER

24 Russell Square

London

First published in 1969
by Faber and Faber Limited
24 Russell Square London WC1
Printed in Great Britain by
Latimer Trend & Co Ltd Plymouth

S.B.N. 571 08577 6

Acknowledgements

I wish to express my thanks to Mrs Carice Elgar Blake for reading and checking my manuscript, giving me permission to quote from her father's works and letters, and allowing me free access to the photographs now housed at the Broadheath museum. The pen and ink cartoons used throughout the book are from Elgar's letters to A. J. Jaeger.

Thanks are also due to Mr Alan Webb, the curator of the Broadheath museum; the staff of the Department of Manuscripts, British Museum; and the Librarian of the Worcester City Library.

Two photographic firms, Geoffrey Hopcraft of Worcester, and Vivian's of Hereford, have been most helpful in preparing the illustrations. The copyright of the pictures of Elgar's birthplace (exterior), and Worcester from the Severn belongs to Mr. Hopcraft. The picture of Elgar's beloved Malvern hills by Anne James is from Ken Russell's fine television documentary on the composer, and is reproduced by kind permission of the BBC. The drawing of the railway bridge at Ludgate Circus is from the Mansell Collection.

With the exception of the extract from *Cockaigne*, which is reproduced by permission of Boosey & Hawkes, the sketch from the Third Symphony (commissioned by the BBC) and the extract from the Sonatina for piano, which is reproduced by permission of Keith Prowse Ltd., all musical examples have been reproduced by kind permission of Novello's, whose copyright they are. The extracts from the two symphonies, the concertos, the piano quintet, and *Falstaff* are here printed in a special reduction prepared by the author.

Contents

Illustrations

Music Examples

Pen and ink drawings used throughout are by Elgar and are from his letters to A. J. Jaeger. These are also reproduced in *Letters to Nimrod*, edited by Percy M. Young, Dobson, 1965.

Elgar

I

The Background

A hundred years ago, when Edward Elgar was a boy, English music was in the doldrums. The long procession of great composers that began in the fifteenth century with John Dunstable and had continued almost without interruption until 1695, when Henry Purcell died, was remembered only in history books. In the hundred and fifty years since Purcell's death there had been little to boast about.

Music, of course, continued to play an important part in English life. There had been composers whose music had given much pleasure in its day. But nobody could pretend that Thomas Augustine Arne and Dr William Boyce loomed as large on the musical horizon as Bach and Handel; that William Sterndale Bennett was the equal of Schumann and Mendelssohn, both of whom had admired and encouraged him; or that the operas of Michael Balfe and William Vincent Wallace matched those of Verdi and Wagner. In the eighteenth and nineteenth centuries English composers may have been men of talent, but they were not men of genius.

Signs of change began to appear while Elgar was at school. In 1862 the young Arthur Sullivan, scarcely more than a schoolboy himself, startled the London musical world with his music for Shakespeare's play *The Tempest*. Four years later he aroused even greater enthusiasm with a symphony, an overture (*In Memoriam*) and a cello concerto.

As it happened, Sullivan was not to win lasting fame with works of this kind, but with the series of light-hearted operettas he wrote with W. S. Gilbert. And it is these delightful entertainments that are the first real proof that something was stirring among English composers.

That 'something' continued to simmer quietly until the end of the century. Sir Hubert Parry and Sir Charles Stanford made their contributions, as did many equally respected but more easily forgotten names. But it was not until 1899 that an English composer was able to produce a work that could be mentioned in the same breath as the music of the great continental masters.

The composer was Edward Elgar. He was forty-two years old. And the work in question, the *Enigma* Variations, revealed that English musical genius had awakened from its two-hundred year slumber, and that the procession of great English composers was to continue, strong and confident and with all its old glory.

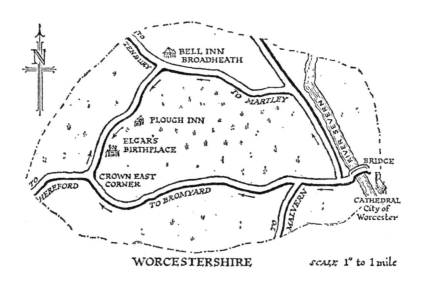

WORCESTERSHIRE   SCALE 1" to 1 mile

II

Boyhood

Edward Elgar was born on 2nd June 1857, at Broadheath, a village some three miles out of Worcester on the road to Tenbury.

The red-brick house in which the Elgar family lived still stands, very much as it was a hundred years ago. Today, however, it is a museum filled with Elgar treasures, visited by music-lovers from all parts of the world. It is not large. Two rooms and a kitchen make up the ground floor, with a narrow staircase leading to a tiny landing and three small bedrooms. Elgar's mother must have found the task of fitting two adults and seven children into so small a space rather like working out a jigsaw puzzle. However much she may have enjoyed the fresh country air, the spacious garden and the view of the splendid Malvern hills, she cannot have been sorry when, in 1860, the whole family moved to a larger house in the city of Worcester itself.

The move was made for business reasons. William Elgar, the composer's father, was a musician. Although born in Dover, he had come to Worcester in 1841 and had there set up a music-shop. A few years later he was joined by his brother Henry, and they ran the shop together as a family business.

It was not long before the name Elgar was well-known in local music circles. William, who played the violin, and Henry, who played the viola, joined in the activities of the Philharmonic Society, the Glee Club and the Instrumental Society. Whenever music was wanted they lent a willing hand —and in the days before gramophone records, radio and television, you may be sure that music-making played an important part in the life of every self-respecting city.

William Elgar was also the organist of St George's Catholic Church—a post he held for nearly forty years. He gave lessons in violin, piano and organ playing, and tuned instruments throughout the county. And, of course, he sold music and instruments in the shop in the High Street. He was just the kind of father a young composer needs.

Worcester, moreover, could offer at least two musical experiences above those of the average provincial city. It had a fine cathedral, where great music could be heard as part of the daily service; and it was a Three Choirs city—that is to say it shared, with Gloucester and Hereford, an annual festival of choral and orchestral music. Each city played host in turn, and had done so since 1724. Composers of world-wide importance thought it an honour to be asked to write works for these occasions, and sometimes they even came to conduct the first performances in person. In choosing his place of birth, Edward Elgar could have done much worse.

From *The Wand of Youth* - Suite No. 2: 'The Tame Bear'

There were few signs in his early days that he was to be a great composer. Unlike the young Mozart he did not start to compose almost before he could talk. He was not even any more anxious to learn to play instruments than other boys of his age. Exploring the twisty streets and alleyways of the old town, and fishing in the River Severn were much more attractive pursuits. Nevertheless he was drawn to music, and because it was part and parcel of the family's whole way of life he began to absorb its lessons almost without knowing.

As soon as he could make a tolerable sound on his violin he joined his father at the meetings of the Worcester Glee Club. Although only twelve, he

Above, two studies of Edward Elgar, aged about thirteen and as a young man; *below*, Broadheath, Worcestershire, Elgar's birthplace

The Elgars' shop in Worcester;
below, the kite enthusiast, from
the BBC/TV film on Elgar

sat with men old enough to be his grandfather, as they smoked their long churchwarden pipes, drank their ale and made music. Soon he was smoking with the best of them.

At home, in the music-shop, he helped behind the counter. When new scores came from the publishers he would glance inside, and then, if something caught his fancy, go on to study them closely. And as the shop was full of instruments he could not help trying them out for himself, just for the fun of it. There were text books to look at—Macfarren's *Rudiments of Harmony*, Cherubini's *Counterpoint*, Crotch's *Elements of Musical Composition*, and dozens more. Everything came under his eager eye. In his own way the young Edward Elgar had begun to give himself as thorough a training in music as would have been available to him anywhere in the country.

He was fortunate in having the kind of mind that can teach itself. When the time came for him to leave school, at the age of fifteen, he plucked up courage to ask his father if the family had enough money to send him to Leipzig. He had heard of the great Conservatoire that Mendelssohn had founded and longed to study there. Hopefully, he had even begun to learn German just in case the miracle came to pass. But it was no use. However much his father might sympathize and try to puzzle a way out, the facts were plain and inescapable: there was no money to spare for even the humblest of musical academies, let alone Leipzig. He would have to go out to work.

He accepted the disappointment with good grace, and in June 1872 allowed himself to be entered as an apprentice in the office of Mr Allen the solicitor. Law was to be his profession.

But it was not easy to put music behind him. He had already begun to compose: songs and short pieces, and even music for a play that he and his brothers and sisters had made up about an imaginary world beyond the stream at the bottom of the garden, from which all bad-tempered grown-ups were definitely barred! With thoughts of this kind floating around in his head, it was impossible to concentrate on dusty legal documents and obscure points of law.

Mr Allen did not try to make him see the error of his ways. The boy worked hard enough, but it was obvious that torts and conveyances held no charm for him. Far better that he should take his chance in the musical world than sit, for ever dissatisfied, on a law-clerk's stool.

In 1873, at the age of sixteen, Edward Elgar took his courage in both hands and declared that he was a musician and that nothing but music would ever bring him happiness.

III

Elgar the Violinist

Elgar began his career as a professional musician by throwing himself wholeheartedly into local musical life. As far as he was concerned there was no music-making so humble that he was prepared to scorn it. He was willing to serve amateurs and professionals alike, for he recognized that every occasion had its lessons and could be put to advantage. Instead of complaining about limited opportunities and the lack of academic training, he set to with a will and turned the musical life of a quiet provincial city into his own private university.

The first step was obvious: he began to help his father in the shop on a full-time basis. The next step was also taken automatically: he was appointed assistant organist to his father at St. George's Church—a matter of formality really, for he had already deputized for him on many occasions. For the rest, he had to shift for himself and rely on his growing reputation as a violinist and good all-round musician.

No one could say that his life at this time was humdrum. He was to be seen playing the bassoon in a wind quintet, along with his brother and three friends. They made the quiet Worcester streets echo to the sound of their music as they serenaded their friends on summer evenings. He was to be seen as the conductor of the Worcester Glee Club, and as the 'efficient leader and instructor' of the newly formed Worcester Instrumental Society. At concerts of the Worcester Philharmonic he had soon outstripped his father, and was to be seen leading the first violins. When festival time came round, there he was in the orchestra, holding his own with men of twice his age and experience. Scarcely a note was played in the entire county that did not, in some way, involve Edward Elgar.

And at the same time he composed and arranged music: for his friends, for the church, for anyone who wanted it. Mostly he was content to write small pieces—songs, dances, trifles for violin and piano—but on at least one occasion he was moved by greater ambitions and attempted a symphony. Wisely he modelled his effort on Mozart's G minor Symphony, imitating its general plan down to the last detail, but using themes of his own. It was an excellent way of learning the secrets of great music.

One very odd appointment came his way. In 1879 he became bandmaster to the orchestra of the County and City of Worcester Pauper Lunatic Asylum. The hospital authorities had come to the enlightened conclusion that music would be soothing and helpful to the patients. Elgar was to train the orchestra, conduct its occasional concerts, and direct the music for a weekly dance. Needless to say, he took the opportunity of slipping in waltzes and quadrilles of his own.

His first public appearance as a composer was equally unusual. In June 1878 the First Worcester Artillery Volunteers announced that they had booked the city's Public Hall and were about to delight everybody with an Amateur Christy Minstrel show. For this rousing occasion—the programme consisted of banjo songs, clog dances and popular part-songs—Elgar provided an *Introductory Overture*. It was much admired. Clearly he was a young man who would go places.

The only place he actually wanted to go to was Leipzig. But this was still out of the question. The income his engagements brought in was very small, and though he saved every penny Leipzig remained as far away as ever. Regretfully he abandoned the idea. Instead, he took himself to London. There, for a little less than eight pounds (half of which went on the rail fare) he enjoyed twelve days of sight-seeing, concert-going and, most important of all, five lessons with the violinist Adolphe Pollitzer. He repeated this kind of educational jaunt whenever he could, with the result that in 1881 the Royal Academy of Music was able to announce that Mr Edward Elgar of Worcester (violin and general musical knowledge) had passed its local examination 'with honours'.

By the time he was twenty-five, Elgar's fame had spread beyond Worcester. He was invited to play in W. C. Stockley's Birmingham orchestra, and this in turn led him to write music which they performed. Again these were trifles, compared with the music he was to write in later years. But composers have to start somewhere, and it was all good training.

This kind of local music-making might have gone on for ever had not two things happened. In 1884 August Manns performed one of Elgar's 'trifles', an orchestral movement called *Sevillana*, at the Crystal Palace in London. And in the following year a London publisher accepted his *Romance* for violin and piano.

Elgar took stock of his position. Was he, after all, more of a composer than a violinist? Was he perhaps wrong to spend so much time and energy trying to become a soloist? The more he considered the matter, the more he realized that he had allowed himself to be side-tracked from his true destiny. The fact that people in the world outside Worcester were prepared to take his compositions seriously made him begin to see himself in a new light. He made up his mind once and for all: henceforth, come what might, he would think of himself as a composer and nothing but a composer.

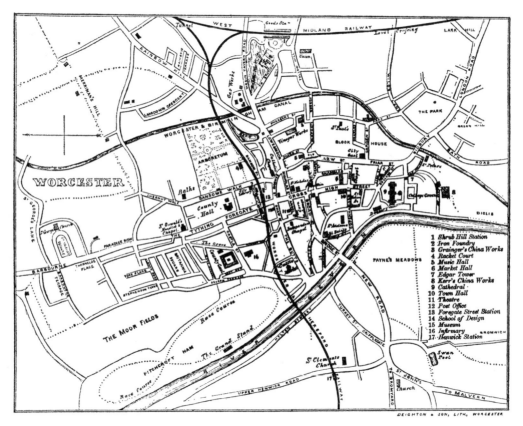

Nineteenth-century street map of Worcester

IV

Elgar the Composer

If anyone living in the neighbourhood of Worcester in the 1880's had asked the question 'Who is the best music-teacher in these parts?', the reply would have come, promptly and decisively, 'Why, Mr. Edward Elgar of course.'

And so it was. Elgar had no difficulty in finding pupils. He was talented, he was young, and considering that he was a musician he was really very gentlemanly. Just the man, in fact, to teach all those young ladies with time on their hands and a taste for music.

One such young lady, Caroline Alice Roberts, began her lessons on 6th October 1886. She took them seriously. She practised far more than she need have done. Even her friends noticed. 'How hard she worked at it', one of them recalled in later years. 'She nearly wore her fingers to the bone practising and I couldn't think what for. She would never have made a fine player'.

Much as she loved music Miss Roberts had no intention of becoming a fine player. The matter was much simpler and much more serious than that: she had fallen in love with her young music-teacher, and it was plain that he returned her feelings. In due course they became engaged, and in 1889 they married.

What would nowadays have been a simple step for anyone to take was not quite so easy for Elgar and Miss Roberts. To begin with, her father had been no less a person than Major-General Sir Henry Gee Roberts, a man of wealth and distinction. Elgar's father was a musician and, worse still, a shop-keeper. Miss Roberts had money of her own—a private income. Elgar had none—not even enough for lessons in Leipzig. And then there was the difference in age. Miss Roberts was eight years older than the man she wished to marry. In the nineteenth-century atmosphere of rigid class distinction and austere social convention these things mattered. The Roberts family protested vigorously.

25

They protested in vain. Caroline Alice had made up her mind. She loved her Edward and had decided not only to marry him, but also to turn him into a great composer. Where others saw only a man of talent, she saw a man of genius.

Encouraged by her faith and determination, Elgar threw up his Worcester appointments. They went to live in London. If he was to be a great composer, this was where opportunity lay. Or so it seemed.

Once in London, however, there proved to be no way of earning a living. Talented musicians were two a penny—instead of pupils looking for teachers, teachers had to search for pupils. And although several publishers agreed to take songs and violin pieces, they offered very little in the way of hard cash for the privilege. There was nothing for it but to return to Worcestershire, the violin and teaching.

They had hardly settled back into the old life when the tide seemed ready to turn again. More pieces were taken for publication, and works began to get performances. They decided to give London a second chance.

This time they stayed for nearly a year, Elgar travelling to Worcester once a week to teach private pupils. And then, ironically, the tide began to flow in the opposite direction. In 1890 the Three Choirs Festival was due to take place in Worcester. The festival committee, seeing that their local boy had begun to make good in the outside world, decided to ask him for a short orchestral work.

The result, the overture *Froissart*, pleased everybody. Even the national press took note, and its critics warmed to the idea that perhaps a new and important talent was emerging. Suddenly the provinces seemed bright and friendly and full of promise. The Elgars, tired of London and discouraged by its competitive stress and strife, decided to return. This time they stayed for more than twenty years.

Among other things, the success of *Froissart* brought Elgar into contact with the publishing house of Novello, who, in the end, were to issue nearly all his major works. The connection was an important one, for Novellos specialized in choral music and it was doubtless this that now turned his thoughts towards cantatas and the vast and hungry sea of English choral societies that were waiting to sing them. During the next eight years he produced five works: *The Black Knight*, *The Light of Life* (an oratorio), *King Olaf*, *The Banner of St. George*, and *Caractacus*. Novellos published them all, and the choral societies snapped them up.

Elgar's early choral music is no worse than the run-of-the-mill stuff that was being written in every English organist's study at this time. Much of it

Chanson de Matin

now seems hopelessly dull—so dull that it is hard to see how it could have been accepted so enthusiastically all over the country. But accepted it was, and it served to raise him from the status of a promising local composer to a composer in whom the whole of England was interested.

By his fortieth birthday Elgar could honestly say that he had reached a position of some importance. Except for the *Serenade* for string orchestra, a handful of 'salon' pieces such as the *Chanson de Matin* (the kind of music that was played in English tea shops and provincial hotels), and possibly the overture *Froissart*, he had, it is true, written nothing by which he is now remembered. But in terms of the late nineteenth century he was a success.

He must, however, have wondered what the future would bring. Compared with most composers he was hopelessly behindhand. Mozart and Schubert had completed their life's work without even reaching the age of forty. Beethoven had written his sixth symphony, and Verdi his nineteenth opera. Even his own contemporaries were streets ahead of him—Richard Strauss, seven years his junior, was already world famous.

How much Elgar's late development was due to the painful way he had been obliged to piece together his musical education, almost without help from anyone, is a matter for speculation. Perhaps a more orthodox training would merely have blunted his very original mind, for when his genius did burst forth it proved to be quite unlike anything that even the greatest of his English contemporaries could produce. Echoing Haydn's words, Edward Elgar might well have said: 'I was cut off from the world, there was no one to confuse or torment me, and so I was forced to become original.'

Elgar's setting of a soccer report he read in a newspaper, which ended with 'He bang'd the leather for goal'—Elgar set it as 'we'.

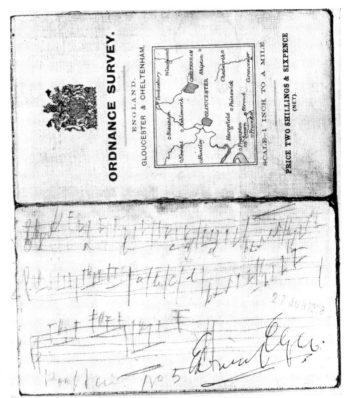

First draft of the main theme for *Pomp and Circumstance March No. 5*; *below*, at work in his study

Elgar's wife;
below, Elgar in June 1900

V

Enigma

With the performance of the *Enigma* Variations on 19th June 1899, Elgar stepped out of the ranks of the talented and took his place among composers of genius. The long apprenticeship was over.

The work had been written during the late autumn of the previous year. The story goes that one evening he began to play something on the piano that his wife had not heard before. She liked it and asked him what it was, but he only replied: 'Nothing. But something might be made of it'. And then he began to improvise, playing the theme in the way he thought some of their friends might have written it. In this way the variations were born.

On the title page of the score Elgar wrote a dedication: 'To my Friends pictured within'. And at the head of each of the fourteen variations he wrote their initials, beginning with his wife's: C.A.E. The final variation he reserved for himself. The whole idea was, he thought, 'distinctly amusing'.

At the first performance, however, he left the audience and the critics to puzzle out the 'meaning' of the work for themselves. This led to complaints, and later he wrote out an explanation to identify each set of initials, so that everyone could appreciate how he had tried to suggest, for example, the bustling impatience of Troyte Griffith (Var VII), the charm and grace of Dorabella (Var X), and the slither of George Robertson Sinclair's dog Dan ('a well-known character') as he fell into the River Wye (Var XI). As for the triumphant finale, it was, he declared, simply to show the world what he intended to do in the future.

One variation stands out, even above the rest of a very remarkable work. It is number IX: Nimrod, the variation for August Jaeger.

Jaeger worked for Novellos. He believed passionately in Elgar's greatness and, at a time when others were doubtful, went out of his way to encourage him. Elgar trusted him implicitly and constantly turned to him for advice. When he died, worn out by ill health and overwork, Elgar wrote:

Enigma

From *Enigma Variations*: IX 'Nimrod'

'Jaeger was for many years the dear friend, the valued adviser and the stern critic of many musicians besides (myself); his place has been occupied but never filled.' He repaid the debt with one of the most beautiful tunes he ever wrote.

The Nimrod variation is also a reminder of the curious delight Elgar took in making mysteries. Instead of putting Jaeger's initials on the score, he preferred a joke. In the Bible Nimrod is described as 'the mighty hunter'. Jaeger was born in Germany, and the German for 'hunter' is 'jaeger'. And so Elgar's title is a riddle—just as his daughter's name, Carice, was a riddle combining syllables of his wife's names (*Car*oline Al*ice*); while in later years his London telegraphic address, Siromoris, was to combine two of his decorations in a palindrome (you can read it forwards *and* backwards and still get Sir and O.M. (Order of Merit).

But the variations contain mysteries that have never been solved, or so it is believed. Elgar himself left a clue, or, rather, posed the problem when he said:

The enigma I will not explain—its 'dark saying' must be left unguessed,

Enigma

From *Enigma Variations*: X 'Dorabella'

From *Enigma Variations*: XI 'G.R.S.'

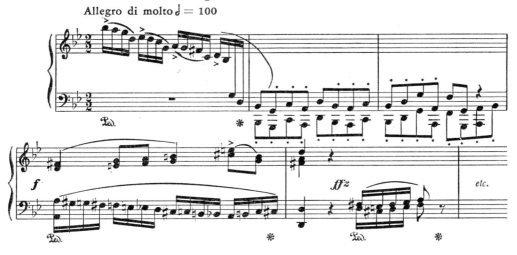

These bars concern G.R.S's bulldog Dan. He falls into the River Wye (bar 1), paddles upstream to find a landing place (bars 2 and 3), and gives a triumphant bark (bar 5). In Elgar's words: 'G.R.S. said, "Set that to music." I did; here it is.'

and I warn you that the apparent connection between the Variations and the Theme is often of the slightest texture; further, through and over the whole set another and larger theme 'goes', but is not played . . . So the principal Theme never appears . . .

And ever since, musicians have been trying to guess the answer.

On the face of it, it looks as if he meant that there is another tune that will 'go' with the theme we hear in the orchestra. Dozens of candidates have been put forward—an American magazine even ran a competition and gave prizes for the best answers—but none of them fit like a glove. Elgar demolished the most promising suggestion by saying: 'No. *Auld lang syne* won't do'. And so the question, if it is a question and not just a brilliant leg-pull on Elgar's part, remains open. Anyone who solves it can be sure of a place in musical history.

Perhaps the real enigma is the one that nobody, not even the composer, could have answered. What was it that suddenly turned Elgar, at the age of forty-two, into a great composer? For with the *Enigma* Variations it is as if a dull, unremarkable chrysalis had broken open, to reveal a splendid butterfly of unimaginable beauty and power. Of all the strange twists in the development of human genius, this is surely one of the most extraordinary.

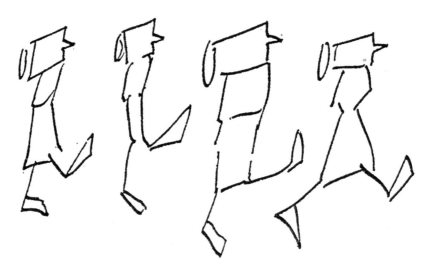

In 1900 Elgar received his Mus.D. His drawing shows
'Philharmonic ladies going to Cambridge for the event'

VI

Gerontius

After the Variations there was more to come. Much more. Within four months the Norwich Festival had given the first performance of a group of songs for contralto and orchestra, *Sea Pictures*. 'Clara Butt dressed like a Mermaid to sing the sea songs at Norwich', was Elgar's cheerful comment. A further token of success came when, for the second time that year, he was commanded to appear before Queen Victoria at Windsor Castle.

Amid all the excitement that accompanied his changing fortunes, Elgar alone remained cool. There was work to do, and he was bursting with ideas. He hid himself in Malvern and set to.

The result of his labours was heard for the first time on 3rd October 1900, at the Birmingham Festival. It was an oratorio, a setting of Cardinal Newman's poem *The Dream of Gerontius*, and the most ambitious thing he had ever tackled.

Everything went wrong at Birmingham. The chorus-master fell ill and died. Stockley, the musician called in to replace him, was seventy years old and past caring about 'new' music. Moreover, although he had been a good friend to Elgar for many years, he found himself out of sympathy with the music—it was so difficult—and the subject—it was so Catholic. The choir was given less than two months to learn the music. It looked so modern that many of them refused point-blank to take it seriously. In any case, they already had more than enough to cope with in learning Parry's *De Profundis*, Coleridge-Taylor's *Hiawatha*, and Bach's *St. Matthew Passion*.

When it came to the performance everybody was tired and resentful. Elgar had agreed to supervise the last rehearsal in person. When he heard the choir sing he was so shocked and disappointed that he could not conceal his feelings. A further rehearsal was agreed for the day before the performance. It went on for six hours, till the singers were ready to drop from ex-

C

From *The Dream of Gerontius*: 'The Angel's farewell'

Andante tranquillo ♪= 92

Soft - ly and gen - tly,____ dear- ly ransomed soul,__ In my most lov- ing arms I now en - fold thee, And, o'er the pen- al__ wa - ters, o'er the pen- al__ wa - ters, as they roll, I poise thee. and I__ low - er thee, and hold thee

34

haustion and had all but lost their voices. Under such conditions the disaster that followed was not surprising.

It is only fair to add that quite a number of critics spoke up for the work and praised it as a 'powerful and profound utterance'. And at least some of Elgar's fellow musicians were convinced it was a masterpiece. The damage was done among the choirmasters and conductors who would normally have leapt at the chance of giving their own performances. A work that was not only too difficult for Birmingham, but also an intense expression of Catholic faith—'it stinks of incense', said Sir Charles Stanford—did not recommend itself. What was needed was someone who would give it the performance it deserved.

The chance came on 19th December 1901. Jaeger had approached Professor Buths of Düsseldorf, showing him the *Enigma* score and arranging for him to hear the Birmingham performance of *Gerontius*. Both works pleased him enormously. He refused to be put off by the fiasco, and promptly arranged to perform them in Germany. This time the success of *Gerontius* was beyond question. And when it was repeated in the following year as part of the Lower Rhine Festival, Richard Strauss publicly declared his faith in Elgar's genius.

After that, of course, the English sat up and took notice. Everybody knew that the only real musicians were foreigners and mostly German. But if one of them could cheerfully announce that an Englishman (an Englishman!) was a great composer, why there must be something in it. Elgar, it was now plain, was a fellow to be taken seriously.

It is perhaps a little difficult for people nowadays to understand how very remarkable *Gerontius* was for its time. Throughout the nineteenth century English composers had been writing oratorios. With Job-like patience they had ransacked the Bible for suitable subjects and then embalmed them in oceans of dreary music, in imitation of the worst moments of Handel and Mendelssohn. A few had been visited by flashes of inspiration; but not for long, and not very often. *Gerontius* was different. It was written with utter conviction and deep passion. It scorned the milk-and-water politeness that passed for music in English academic circles. It was operatic in its intensity. It burned with life and vitality.

And this is why Elgar is so important to the music of England. His greatest works shout for joy and weep without shame in a way that English music had not dared to do for two hundred years. Elgar, the man who never went near a Public School or a University, who was spared Protestant good taste and well-bred piety, the man who had gone his own way, fighting for every inch of ground, was, perhaps for these very reasons, the man who alone could show English music the way back to its former greatness. He touched the secret spring of English musical genius and opened the door to everything we enjoy today.

The disappointment of the Birmingham performance of *Gerontius*, however, wounded Elgar deeply. On the last page of the manuscript he had copied some words of John Ruskin:

> This is the best of me. For the rest, I ate, I drank, I slept, I loved, I hated as another. My life was as a vapour, and is not. But this is what I saw, and know. This, if anything of mine, is worth your memory.

Gerontius was his confession of faith, and to hear it for the first time in a faltering, barely understood performance was something he found hard to forget or forgive. Even its later success did not console him. In the depths of gloom he wrote to Jaeger: 'As far as I am concerned music in England is dead . . .' For a moment he seriously considered giving up altogether.

Fortunately the mood passed. The cheerful side of his nature reasserted itself and he picked up his pen once more.

Ludgate Circus, London, in the 1890s

Three views of Worcester from the River Severn: *above*, Worcester in the eighteenth century; *right*, a postcard from Elgar showing Worcester Cathedral; *below*, a twentieth-century view of the Severn Bridge and the Cathedral

Above, one of Elgar's many cartoons, May 1910; *below*, an extract from one of Mozart's letters which Elgar copied and kept on his desk.

Ween 1781

x x x the passions, whether violent or otherwise, must never be expressed to disgust, — and music, even in the most terrific situation, never give pain to the ear, but ever delight it and remain Music.

W. A. Mozart.

(Letter to his father)

VII

Success and Honours

The works that followed *Gerontius* are of a very different character and contrast strongly with it. They are every bit as masterly and just as alive; but instead of illuminating inward, spiritual matters, they are concerned with the bustle and pageantry of the everyday world. For a time at least, Elgar put aside the feelings of the poet and assumed instead the guise of military bandmaster.

The first of these new, exuberant works was heard in June 1900. It was an overture, and Elgar had christened it *Cockaigne*—adding, as a subtitle, 'In London Town' just to make his meaning clear. According to the poets of the Middle Ages, Cockaigne was a land that flowed with milk and honey, where the houses were made of barley sugar and the streets paved with pastry; it was a land of luxury and good-fellowship—even the shops gave their goods away.

Elgar's musical portrait of London is just as magical, even though the sugar and pastry must now be thought of, to use his own words, as 'stout and steak'. It is all bustle and excitement, noise and good humour; with bands marching and flags waving and crowds cheering—in short: all the grandeur and magnificence of the heart of a great Empire at the height of its power. Nor does Elgar forget the sudden aspects of peace and quiet and beauty that are to be found, when you least expect them, even in the middle of London's tumult. It is hardly surprising that the work was a success: the average Englishman felt that Edward Elgar had found music to explain what England was all about.

In October the same year further confirmation came with the two *Pomp and Circumstance* marches. 'Listen to this,' said Elgar. 'This'll make 'em sit up.' It did. One of the tunes, with words added, rapidly became a popular song: *Land of Hope and Glory*. There were even proposals that it should be adopted as the National Anthem.

Many people nowadays find this side of Elgar rather hard to swallow.

37

From *Cockaigne*: 'In London Town'

38

'Such music,' they say, 'is bombastic and vulgar and full of the worst kind of empty-headed patriotism.' In one sense they are right, and Elgar himself admitted as much when he said:

I like to look on the composer's vocation as the old troubadours and bards did. In those days it was no disgrace for a man to be turned on to step in front of an army and inspire them with a song. For my part I know that there are a lot of people who like to celebrate events with music. To those people I have given tunes. Is that wrong?

But to complain is to misunderstand the period. The time was ripe for exuberance. Tarrying just a little longer than the century to which she had given her name, Queen Victoria had at last died. A new century, and in 1901 a new King—a bluff, good-humoured man who enjoyed life and expected others to enjoy it also. The Edwardian age saw the climax of England's power as a nation and an Empire. Vast areas on the map of the world were coloured a reassuring British red. Her sailors ruled the seas, and a glimpse of her soldiers' uniforms was enough to quell even the thought of revolution. Her industries were the most powerful the world had yet seen, and her wealth was enormous.

All this the Edwardian age celebrated, like a sumptuous and final banquet before the First World War scattered the magnificence forever. Few ages have been so confident and felt so secure. While the Pax Britannica held, what could possibly go wrong? The Edwardians celebrated, and Elgar, a man of his time, celebrated too.

If there is any problem, it is the problem Elgar himself had to face: how to reconcile the 'popular' side of his nature with the deeper, contemplative moods he was also capable of. Part of his greatness lies in the fact that his finest works strike the necessary balance, and thus produce music that is both sturdy and imaginative. Works of genius are not made out of cobwebs, such as can be blown away by the merest breath. Rather, they are spun from steel—a dependable material which can still achieve gossamer fineness. Elgar in his music was simply himself: sometimes vulgar and noisy, often quiet, tender and deeply moving—you cannot separate the two.

Even though it never brought him much financial reward, Elgar's success with the public grew during the early years of the century. Long before he had become Master of the King's Musick he had been accepted as *the* English composer, the man to be turned to on all important occasions. The process of turning him into a national institution had begun.

Honours followed one another as a matter of course. The University of Cambridge made him a Doctor of Music in 1900, and in the years that followed no fewer than eight universities offered similar tributes. An all-Elgar festival was held at Covent Garden in 1904, with the King and Queen in attendance—an unprecedented occasion in England. In the same year he was invited to become a member of the Athenaeum Club, as 'a person of distinguished eminence.' And then, in July, he was made a knight. After that the honours came thick and fast—including, in 1911, the coveted Order of Merit. He became Master of the King's Musick in 1924, and was made a baronet in 1931. Few composers have been so thoroughly applauded in their lifetime.

VIII

The Years of Greatness

With the exception of a handful of works written immediately after the First World War, nearly everything by which Elgar is now remembered was composed between 1898 and 1913. Fifteen years is not long, but in that time Elgar set a new standard for English music and laid foundations upon which future generations were to build with increasing confidence and success.

He worked his revolutions quite casually and without fuss. The *Introduction and Allegro* for string orchestra came out in 1905 and was successful, but no special claims were made for it. Yet, in terms of English music, it is a model of advanced string writing and set a new standard which other composers would have to take into account.

It is not an easy work, as any orchestral player will tell you; but it is written with such an intimate understanding of what strings can do that it almost plays itself. This is one of the great secrets about all Elgar's orchestral music. During the years of toil as a humble member of orchestras in and around Worcester, he had learned to know music *from within*. He knew exactly what instruments could be asked to do, and precisely how they could be made to sound at their best. His scores are therefore miracles of commonsense and practicality, full of tiny details which help the music to sing. And however hard he may drive them, few orchestral players have ever had to complain that Elgar has made unreasonable demands.

At the time of writing the *Introduction and Allegro* he was a worried man. In November 1904 the University of Birmingham had pressed him to become their first Professor of Music. The position had, in fact, been created specially for him; and so, when it was offered, he had no real option but to accept. Besides, he was short of money—success only seemed to result in expenses that far outweighed any increase in income.

Interesting though his lectures were, they were not happy. He had an unfortunate knack of saying things about English music that hurt some of his less gifted colleagues. It was no help at all that what he said was true—if anything it only made matters worse. The realization of what he had done, of course, threw him into the deepest gloom and even made it impossible to write music. After one lecture he murmured to a friend: 'I must go and buy some strychnine. This is the end of me.'

Fortunately the depression did not last (any more than the professorship, which he resigned in 1907), and he was able to take up music again. Three works occupied him between 1902 and 1906: an overture, *In the South* (*Alassio*), written as a momento of an Italian holiday; and the two oratorios: *The Apostles* and *The Kingdom*, which were intended as parts of a trilogy. The third part, *The Last Judgement*, was never completed—hardly begun, even.

The new oratorios were not as successful as Elgar had hoped. However shy English choirs may have been of *Gerontius* to begin with, they soon took it to their hearts. With *The Apostles* and *The Kingdom* the process worked in reverse. They were both accepted with enthusiasm at the start, and then gradually dropped. Their fate almost completely discouraged Elgar from writing large-scale choral works—*The Music Makers* (1912) is the only piece of any significance to follow them.

What really interested him now was orchestral music. He began by arranging some of the pieces he had written in his youth into two orchestral suites, which he called *The Wand of Youth*. All the pieces have fanciful titles, and at least one of them, 'Fairies and Giants', had been written as long ago as 1867, when he was only ten; but of course, he now gave it the added polish of forty years' experience.

Getting *The Wand of Youth* together must have been a pleasant relaxation from the serious work he had in hand. This was nothing less than the composition of a symphony, and it occupied him throughout 1907 and most of the following year.

In fact he had been toying with the idea of such a work since 1898, and at various times during the next few years had reported that some kind of progress had been made. Several famous conductors had allowed themselves to get excited, and at least two festivals looked forward to giving the first performance. But Elgar's composing methods were peculiar. He would sketch out a few bars here and a few bars there, all from different parts of different movements—rather as if he had a vague outline of the entire work in his head, but was uncertain of the details. To finish a composition meant piecing all the fragments together so that they flowed in one continuous, effortless stream of music. Presumably the bits and pieces of this early

From Symphony No. 1 in A flat: 1st movement

From Symphony No. 2 in E flat: 4th movement

43

symphony stubbornly refused to fit into a pattern and so had to be abandoned.

At all events, the symphony which had its first performance at Manchester on 3rd December 1908 was completely new and showed no signs of awkwardness. Its success was enormous. And when it was repeated four days later in London, bookings were so heavy that an extra performance had to be arranged for the same week. In its first year it was performed nearly a hundred times in England alone. When Richter began the first Manchester rehearsal by saying: 'Gentlemen, let us now rehearse the greatest symphony of modern times, written by the greatest modern composer . . .', adding under his breath, 'and not only in this country', he was only anticipating what everybody was soon to feel. With his Symphony No 1 in A flat, Elgar hit the nail on the head.

He decided to celebrate by taking a holiday from music, and promptly devoted himself to chemistry—rigging up a hut in the garden (they were now living in Hereford) which he christened 'The Ark'. On one famous occasion he even managed to blow up a water butt, much to the consternation of his wife and neighbours. It was not only music-lovers that were pleased when he eventually began composing again.

These were happy and fruitful years. Close on the heels of the first symphony came the Concerto in B minor for violin and orchestra (1910), the Symphony No 2 in E flat (1911), and the symphonic poem *Falstaff* (1913). All three were masterpieces.

Only one thing cast a shadow over the scene. In May 1909 August Jaeger died. He had been Elgar's closest friend and most trusted adviser. The loss was irreparable.

Nimrod's theme

44

Sir Edward Elgar aged about seventy-five

A rough draft of the unfinished
Third Symphony; *below*, Master
of the King's Musick, 1932

IX

The War Years

Elgar, as we have seen, reached the height of his powers in the years immediately preceding the First World War. Behind him, like milestones in the history of English music, lay a series of masterpieces that could hold their own against all comers. But however modern they may have appeared to his fellow-countrymen, these works belonged, in reality, to the dying tradition of nineteenth-century romanticism. Along with Richard Strauss, Mahler and Fauré, Elgar represented a final blaze of romantic splendour. Although he gave English composers the confidence to be great, he did not point the path they would travel. The future did not lie in his music.

This, of course, is not to say that anything was wrong with it. Many great composers have been conservative in their attitudes, and concerned themselves with bringing an accepted style to perfection—Bach is the obvious example. Not everybody is required to be a pioneer.

Elgar's music is laid out on a vast scale. The symphonies, for example, last nearly an hour each, and the violin concerto occupies the best part of forty-five minutes. They are works that unfold slowly, to reveal a wealth of tunes over which he lingers lovingly. They call for vast orchestras, and then proceed to revel in the most sumptuous effects of harmony and orchestration.

The mood of his music is a mixture of the heroic and the melancholy. Time and time again you will find the word 'nobilmente' written as a direction to urge the players to bring out the nobility and splendour of his great rolling tunes. Time and time again you will find that these tunes consist of repeated phrases (sequences), rising and falling in pitch and thus designed to squeeze the last drop of emotion from the original idea. Time and time again you will hear echoes of military music and ceremonial pageantry, and then hear it melt into something wistful and tear-laden. In short: Elgar's music says grand things in the grand manner and always wears its heart on its sleeve.

From *Violin Concerto*: opening of 1st movement

46

These are not popular qualities nowadays. We may still listen to such music and enjoy it, but no modern composer would feel moved to write anything similar for himself. We live in a very different age, and our music, in consequence, stands for very different things. It is important to bear this in mind when thinking about Elgar and his career, for the change of attitude began in his own lifetime, and he was faced with the problem of being out of date long before his creative life was over.

The First World War, of course, was the physical event that forced the change on Europe. Nineteenth-century attitudes, in particular the feeling that life was secure and well-ordered, lingered on well into the twentieth century. The pattern did not change obligingly at the stroke of midnight on the last day of the old century. But it did change in the horror and misery of trench warfare. After that experience it was impossible to look at the world in the same light.

Elgar spent the war years mostly in London. He had moved there in 1912, to an elegant house in Hampstead which his wife felt was more in keeping with his acknowledged importance. 'Severn House', as it was called, just to remind him of his beloved West country, was delightful, even if it was a little too expensive. He soon settled down to work.

With the declaration of war he found that, unwittingly, he had written one of the great 'war songs' of the day. 'Land of Hope and Glory', which, as we have seen, was merely the trio from the first *Pomp and Circumstance* march with words added, was on everybody's lips. Audiences rose to their feet whenever it was played. They sang it in the streets. Elgar, its innocent composer, became a kind of national hero.

The War Years

It was typical of him that he now put aside what he called 'peace music', and threw himself into the composition of deliberately patriotic works. They are no longer performed, for their effectiveness depended very much on the mood of the times, but they were received with open arms. This, and his duties as Staff-Inspector in the Hampstead Special Constabulary (he was 0015014), was part of his contribution to war work.

On the surface it would seem that everything was well with Elgar. He was successful and honoured and, for once, reasonably wealthy. But as the war went on he became immensely troubled and sad. So many of his friends had been German, and he owed so much of his success to Germany. It was unbearable to see the bitterness grow and enmity deepen. All the civilized values that he and his generation had cherished now seemed to dissolve. The world, he saw quite plainly, would never be the same again.

Perhaps this is why the last great works he wrote—the string quartet (1918), the piano quintet (1918) and the Concerto in E minor for cello and orchestra (1919)—are filled with sadness and regret. They are quiet works. In them the heroic side of his imagination is played down, subdued to a ghostly echo and shot through with melancholy. They are intensely moving.

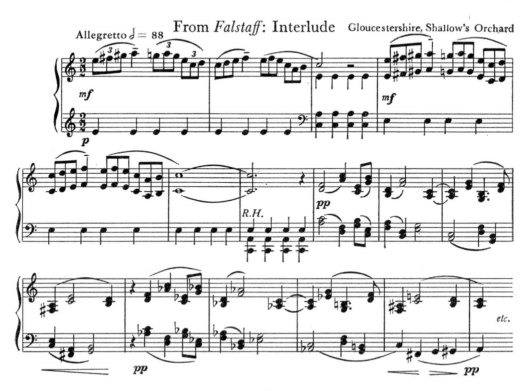

From *Falstaff*: Interlude   Gloucestershire, Shallow's Orchard

The War Years

These works were not composed at 'Severn House', but at 'Brinkwells', a cottage near Fittleworth in Sussex that Lady Elgar had found in 1917. To Elgar, 'sick of towns', it was an enchanted place, with a river near by and walks in abundance. By the autumn of 1919 he had decided that 'Severn House' should be sold and London left for ever.

But events moved faster than his plans. In April 1920, Lady Elgar fell ill and, within a few days, died. From that moment, so far as Edward Elgar was concerned, music was dead too.

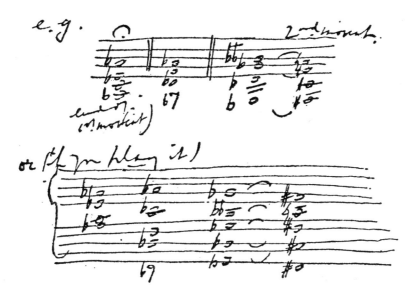

Elgar demonstrating a point in his harmony to Jaeger

X

The Years of Retirement

Although he was to live for another fourteen years, Elgar could scarcely bring himself to compose after his wife's death. A few songs, a march or two, incidental music to a couple of plays, a number of orchestral trifles: what he completed amounts to very little, either in quantity or in quality. It was as if everything he had done had been done for her. And now, the inspiration gone, he could see no point in continuing the struggle. Her death, and the fact that the world was a very different place from the world his music had celebrated, left him with nothing to say—nothing that was worth saying.

He was still, however, an important figure in music and much revered. But when he conducted performances of his own works, or appeared at music festivals, it was as if the ghost of some classical master had stepped out of the past. Elgar in the 1920s was already a legend.

The fact that he now spent more and more time at his London clubs and was often to be seen backing his fancy on the racecourse, did not help matters. In such surroundings, hobnobbing with royalty and the aristocracy, he could easily be mistaken for some retired colonel or country squire. The sillier kind of critics concluded that this was the real Elgar and that his music must likewise be 'old bufferish' and unworthy of attention.

What he was doing, of course, was simply to hide behind a conventional mask in order to protect the sensitive part of his nature from intruders. He had never, at any time, been very communicative about his music and what it meant to him. Now more than ever he found it necessary to withdraw into his shell.

In 1929 he moved into his last home: a house on Rainbow Hill, just outside Worcester. And here a flicker of interest in composing began to return. He wrote the *Severn Suite*, a test piece for the annual brass band contest at the Crystal Palace. A year later he completed another suite, a *Nursery Suite* which he dedicated to Their Royal Highnesses the Princesses Elizabeth and Margaret Rose.

And then, in 1932, it was announced that he was at work on a new symphony. The man behind the inspiration was George Bernard Shaw. They had been friends for many years, and Elgar now wished to celebrate their friendship in a major work. Shaw, moreover, desperately keen that Elgar should begin composing in earnest again, had bullied the BBC into offering a handsome commission fee for just such a work. Elgar joyfully accepted the challenge.

From *Cello Concerto*: 3rd movement

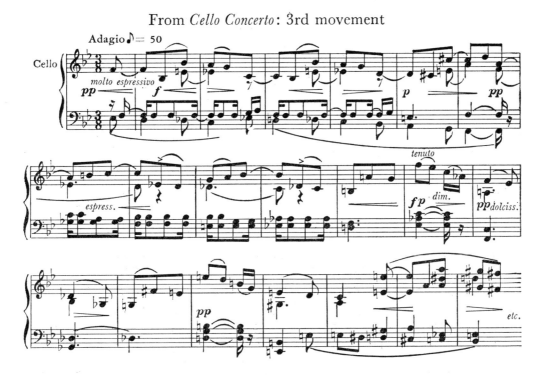

His reawakened interest soon spread to the idea of writing an opera, and by 1933 both this and the symphony were beginning to take shape.

He set about his work in the usual way, writing a passage here and a passage there—dozens of fragments that he would later be able to knead together into a complete composition. There is enough evidence, in the shape of precisely such bits and pieces, to suggest that what had happened to Elgar in 1932 was a genuine return of creative activity and that, given time, both the opera and the symphony would have been successfully completed.

But time was not given. In April 1933 he began to feel pain. It was diagnosed as sciatica. But the doctors were too optimistic, and in October the same year he was rushed into hospital and operated upon for what was now clearly a malignant tumour. The operation came too late—his life could be prolonged for a few months, but not saved.

When he was strong enough he moved back to his Worcester home. In January 1934 he was able to supervise the recording of music from *Caractacus*. Engineers set up a microphone and loudspeaker in his bedroom, connecting them by GPO land lines to the recording studio in London. The London Symphony Orchestra rehearsed. He listened, criticized their interpretation and thanked them. Then they recorded the work and played it back. It was his last contact with the musical world.

He knew he was dying. As the days wore on and he became weaker, he grew increasingly worried about the symphony he would never finish. No one would understand it, it was all bits and pieces. His friend, W. H. Reed, standing by the bedside heard him say: 'Don't let anyone tinker with it . . . no one could understand . . . no one must tinker with it.' A promise was given, and the symphony remains, to this day, exactly as he left it.

It was a quarter to eight in the morning when he died, on 23rd February 1934. The man who had been born in a tiny cottage, in a remote Worcester village, was mourned by the whole of the music-loving world.

Theme from the unfinished Third Symphony

XI

The Fate of his Music

The story of a great composer does not end with his funeral and the last neat obituary. What happens to his music in the years that follow is as important as the events of his life, and often just as exciting. For then that music has to make its own way in the world. As the years go by, there will be fewer and fewer people to help simply because they have known and admired the man who wrote it. In the end, it will remain in existence simply because of its merits. And it will often be the case that the qualities that have kept it alive will be precisely those that were not at first apparent. In one sense, then, the true story of Elgar and his music began on 23rd February 1934.

Like all composers who have won popularity during their lifetime, Elgar's music went into eclipse during the years immediately after his death. The tendency to underestimate his achievement, and even pour scorn on it, began several years before he died. As early as 1930, the eminent musicologist Edward J. Dent, writing from his lofty position as professor of music at Cambridge University, declared that Elgar's music was 'too emotional and not quite free from vulgarity . . . pompous in style . . . dry and academic. . . .' Four years later even a sympathetic critic, the composer Constant Lambert, felt impelled to write: 'much of Elgar's music, through no fault of its own, has for the present generation an almost intolerable air of smugness, self-assurance and autocratic benevolence'. Thereafter, and for nearly twenty-five years, the process of misunderstanding continued.

He was not entirely forgotten. *The Dream of Gerontius* remained popular with choral festivals, and the *Enigma* variations held a place in the concert-hall. Few tea-shop trios could exist for long without playing the *Chanson de Matin*, and no patriotic occasion was complete without the massed singing of *Land of Hope and Glory*. But almost everything else was ignored. The First Symphony, which had run to nearly a hundred performances in the first year of its existence, was rarely played, and the Second Symphony and

53

From *Piano Quintet:* opening of 2nd movement

Cello Concerto scarcely ever. And for all the attention it received, his chamber music might never have been written.

Neglect was, perhaps, inevitable. When a man's music has embodied the age in which he lived, it is to be expected that succeeding generations will react against it.

Moreover, in England the situation was particularly unfavourable. Elgar had proved beyond doubt that English musical genius had come to life again. But he had composed in the German style. He was part of the tradition that included Brahms, Mahler, and Richard Strauss. And even though he spoke with an unmistakably English accent, the basis of his musical language was German through and through.

The great English composers who followed him, Holst and Vaughan Williams, felt uncomfortable in this tradition. It stifled them, and in the end they rejected it—turning, instead, to English folk-song. In the light of their discoveries, Elgar's achievement suddenly seemed tame and traditional.

Nor were musical events on the Continent any more sympathetic. After the First World War a complete reaction set in against romantic music. What now mattered was music that was elegant, witty and sharp-edged, often bitingly percussive and dissonant; music that avoided, at all costs, the grand romantic manner. Soon Hollywood was to seize upon the tattered remains of romantic music, driving it further and further into disrepute.

Attitudes to romantic music, and to Elgar in particular, did not begin to change until the 1960s. And then, suddenly, everything seemed to happen at once. His music had always held a place in the gramophone record catalogues (he was, after all, one of the first great composers to leave authoritative accounts of his own music—he began recording in 1914), but now recordings began to appear that showed a new insight into his music, revealing qualities that had been glossed over by years of neglect and misunderstanding. Young artists began to discover Elgar for themselves—the extraordinary impact made by the twenty-year-old Jacqueline du Pré with the Cello Concerto is a case in point. The BBC sponsored a film about his life from a young and highly gifted director, Ken Russell. His approach was fresh and imaginative, and the result delighted millions of viewers. The sale of Elgar records promptly rocketed, and concert promoters began to look upon his name with favour once more. Works that had hitherto been ignored—*The Music Makers*, and the chamber music, for example—were taken out again and found to be good.

Such changes, together with the undeniably helpful fact that the Victorian and Edwardian ages have come to look remarkably secure and attractive

55

when compared with our own troubled time, have brought about a new evaluation of Elgar and his music. After thirty years in the wilderness he has been reborn. Now, for the first time, he can be seen clearly, in the context of musical history: a representative of his age, and a worthy member of a great tradition.

*spur.

a knight.

XII

Elgar the Man

Many books have been written about Elgar's life and music, but it is only in recent years that any convincing attempts have been made to understand the very unusual nature of his genius. What most people have been content with is Elgar the Public Monument—the version of his life and character, neat, tidy, and beyond reproach, that well-meaning friends and popular superstition have contributed as the only possible picture of a Great Man.

When Elgar's music was in eclipse it was customary to dismiss it on account of its hearty, 'pomp and circumstance' qualities. It does have these qualities, and they are a true reflection of one side of his nature, but this is not the only side.

Unfortunately, Elgar rather chose to play up the no-nonsense, John Bullish part of his character, especially in his dealings with the public. He moved in society and the world of London clubs. He appeared to take a greater interest in race meetings than in music. Tall and distinguished, he might have been a military man.

Yet if you looked closely, as the young violinist W. H. Reed was to recall in his book about Elgar, it became obvious that the military bearing was no more than a façade, a mask behind which the sensitive artist could hide:

'It was his eyes perhaps that gave the clue to his real personality: they sparkled with humour, or became grave or gay, bright or misty as each mood in the music revealed itself. His hands, too, gave another clue: they were never still even when he was not conducting . . . they were always eloquent, always saying something. . . .'

Far from practising any English restraint, Elgar's private attitude to music was positive and extremely emotional. 'If you cut that it would bleed,' he said about a passage that particularly pleased him. He wrote nothing that was anaemic or half-hearted. His music may not always have been first rate, but at least it was always alive. Critics, quite rightly, have complained that he

57

did not always discriminate, that he could be noisy, vulgar and sentimental. But it is precisely this refusal to shelter behind 'good taste' that enabled him to rise also to the heights.

Even if his music did not make it crystal clear, it would be obvious from his letters that Elgar was a man of extreme and quick-changing moods. On the one hand we have the Elgar of jokes and riddles, brimming over with schoolboy 'japes' and noisy good humour—the Elgar who would tease his friend Jaeger:

Creature!

Cease reviling mine instruments: there are only three bangs on the GONG in the whole of Caractacus and I'll wager a pound to a bang you can't tell where they are—so artfully are they dispersed. Yah!

Let's call it, as in 8vo score—

The Roman Triumph (March) eh?

it's handy for programmes; see?

March . . . 'The Roman Triumph' . . . (Caractacus) Jaeger.

But his mood could as easily change to one of complete despair, and then Jaeger would receive:

No thank you: I really cannot afford it [to accept a non-paying commission] and am at the end of my financial tether. Don't go and tell anyone but I *must* earn money somehow—I *will not* go back to teaching and I think I must try some trade—coal agency or houses—I really wish I were dead over and over again but I dare not, for the sake of my relatives, do the job myself. Well we shall see—I've not read the papers yet re Gerontius and never shall now. I'm sorry you've been bothered over it—just my influence on everything and everybody—always evil!

Both these letters, and dozens like them, can be read in Dr Young's two collections. They do not bear out the old, complacent public image.

Once you have learned to look beneath the surface pomp and circumstance, the most striking quality in Elgar's music is its deep melancholy. It is not the music of self-pity—the sadness goes deeper than that.

Striking evidence of Elgar's attitude to life and music can be seen in his setting of Arthur O'Shaughnessy's poem *The Music Makers*. The music is full of self-quotations—the *Enigma* theme and the *Nimrod* variation, in particular—which, because they are now allied to words, serve to underline exactly what his music meant to him. Elgar was drawn to the words, and set them as he did, precisely because they had this autobiographical significance.

From *The Music Makers*

Elgar the Man

We are the music-makers,
And we are the dreamers of dreams,
Wandering by lone sea-breakers,
And sitting by desolate streams;
World-losers and world-forsakers,
On whom the pale moon gleams:
Yet we are the movers and shakers
Of the world for ever, it seems.

The more we consider the facts of Elgar's career, the more extraordinary they must seem. He enjoyed no formal education in music, and was backed by no university or college. At a time when social position counted, even in music, he was a penniless upstart from the provinces. He might easily have remained, like his brother Frank, behind the counter of the family music shop. But he became one of the greatest English composers and entered the highest ranks of society.

Yet when he looked around and saw the comfortable careers carved out by 'composers' who had enjoyed every social and educational advantage but scarcely had a hundredth part of his talent, he could not help feeling angry and bitter. At the back of his mind there lingered the suspicion that he had missed something, and that his career had been held back and his development stultified. In his letters and, occasionally, in his more unguarded public statements (the Birmingham lectures, for example) the mask slips and the anguish shows itself for a moment.

Probably he was wrong. Without the struggle and heartache, the strength and determination that distinguishes his music might never have shown itself. Had there been nothing to fight against, he might easily have become what the majority of his English contemporaries were: complacent, gentlemanly, and unmemorable.

Enigma Postscript

While this book was in the press, Mr. Michael Kennedy published a remarkable study: *Portrait of Elgar*. In it he points out that one of the first critics of the *Enigma* Variations, Arthur Johnstone, believed that the 'larger theme', teasingly referred to by Elgar, was in fact 'the temperament of the artist, through which he sees his subjects; for that, and nothing else, is what forms the connecting link between any series of portraits by the same hand'.

Mr. Kennedy then points out that in a letter to Dorabella (Mrs. Richard Powell) Elgar signs the first four notes of the *Enigma* theme instead of his name. (Actually he does this twice. It occurs again in the facsimile letter of 10th October 1901, printed as part of Mrs. Powell's book, *Edward Elgar, memories of a variation*.) These four notes fit the words Edward Elgar in the most natural way:

Ed-ward El – gar

And so, perhaps, it is Elgar's own name that 'goes' throughout the work and is the unheard theme.

Thinking therefore along these lines, it would seem possible to regard the entire work as a portrait of the composer. Elgar the lonely artist as the theme itself (note that he uses it in precisely this context in *The Music Makers*), and Elgar in relation to his friends as the variations that follow—for every person changes slightly according to the company he finds himself in. The Finale, an indication of what Elgar intended to achieve through his music, then follows quite naturally. The complete work would thus read: the composer as he is in his innermost self; the composer as he appears in company with his friends; the composer as he one day will be.

From Sonatina for piano: I

Suggestions for Further Reading

Although several books have been written about Elgar and his music, nothing has yet appeared that can be considered a 'definitive' study. For general purposes the most useful volumes are:

Edward Elgar, *His Life and His Music*, by Diane McVeagh (Dent, 1955)

Elgar O.M., by Percy M. Young (Collins, 1955)

Letters of Edward Elgar, edited by P. M. Young (Bles, 1956)

Letters to Nimrod, edited by P. M. Young (Dobson, 1965)

Portrait of Elgar, by Michael Kennedy (Oxford, 1968)

Two further volumes, now out of print, throw interesting light on Elgar's relationship with his friends:

Elgar as I Knew Him by William H. Reed (Gollancz, 1936)

Edward Elgar, Memories of a Variation, by Mrs. Richard Powell (O.U.P., 1936, reprinted 1947)

Summary List of Elgar's Works

Choral Works with Orchestra:
    The Black Knight (cantata), 1893
    The Light of Life (oratorio), 1896
    Caractacus (cantata), 1898
    The Dream of Gerontius (oratorio), 1900
    The Apostles (oratorio), 1903
    The Kingdom (oratorio), 1906
    The Music Makers (choral ode), 1912

Large Orchestral Works:
    Variations on an original theme ('Enigma'), 1899
    Pomp and Circumstance marches, 1–5, 1901–30
    Cockaigne (In London Town) Overture, 1901
    Introduction and Allegro (string orchestra), 1905
    In the South (Alassio) overture, 1903
    Symphony No 1, in A flat major, 1908
    Symphony No 2, in E flat major, 1911
    Falstaff: symphonic study, 1913

Concertos:
    Concerto for violin and orchestra, 1910
    Concerto for cello and orchestra, 1919

Chamber Music:
    String Quartet in E minor, 1918
    Quintet in A minor (piano and strings), 1918
    Sonata in E minor (violin and piano), 1918

Index

65

Index